Acknowledgements:
Red Wolf Press Australia, and the Author greatly acknowledge the following people in the creation of this work; Esther Coultas, Jonathan Ratcliffe, Lish Skec, George Ghio, Catherine Zickgraf and Gene Barry.

Recent Publications:
The Preludes James WF Roberts
Trapped in the Bell Jar (Gore journal vol 4)
Ten Poems
Red Wolf Press Australia.
Blue Electric Dusk
(first folio collection. Numen Books 213)

Websites:
http://boneorchardpoetry.blogspot.com.au/2013/08/
Anthologies:
Short Fiction:
Slaughter House vol. 3:
Serial Killer ed. Siren's Call Pub. (USA) 2013
Poetry:
The Art of Being Human/
Sagittarius—Love Poems Vol: 6 (Romania) (2013)
The Art of Being Human Vol: 3 (Romania) (2013)
Melpomene Anthology: Poetry. Numen Books 2012.
Page Seventeen: Busybird publishing. (Aus) 2012
Song of Sahel: Ebook for African Drought relief (UK) 2012
Painted Words 2012 (Bendigo Tafe)
Spirit of Poe: Charitable Anthology Literary Landmark Press(USA). 2011/12
Verandah Twenty-Seven. Deakin University 2011.

About the Author:
James WF Roberts/Red Wolf
is a radio presenter on Phoenixfm Bendigo www.phoenixfm.org.au,
is regular feature on the Melbourne poetry scene.and is poetry curator and editor of Red Wolf Press Australia
http://redwolfpressaustralia.blogspot.com.au/

With Love for Esther Coultas.
Majority of work was done between 1st October 2013-Sept 1 2014

Many Truths of an Absurd Nature

James WF Roberts

For Her

1. Many Truths Of An Absurd Nature

the mirror lies,
the bottle denies
the very truth we seek.
Photos fade
mind decays
would you rather be
mighty, rich or meek?
Strong or weak,
fast or slow
just sit back
and let nature flow.

Presumed guilty
from the day we're born
will my saintly nature show
before the dawn?

will your ancient beauty end
before I reach the climax of this song?
is a sunflower the cosmos?
have you come here to witness
how all of it will be lost?

singing songs of old
sharing stories never meant to be told
Lying here in the womb of night
only memories of us, shall bask in the light.
Morning commute
dullness of life
how much of this fabric
can we unpick with a knife?

toy monkeys endless rows of
grey drab men in grey drab suits
football long ago replaced
the need for salvation and church.
Wisdom walks the streets tonight
now she goes by Desiree
trading her promises for flesh.

Jesus sits at home and self-harms
then masturbates.

Buddha owns a brokerage firm,
G-d's down a back alleyway,
shooting up again.

Mohammed betrayed decades ago
for a throne, Rolls Royce's, automatic
rifles—and a fuck tonne of oil.

Traffic never stops,
no-one ever has any place to go.
Always within reach of mass media
and your phone.

Ignorant of beauty
unless it's on the magazine rack.
Single men are creepy,
single women sad and lonely.
Celebrity is bliss.
celibacy a parlour trick.
Strap me into the machines
turn it on—wipe me clean,
let oblivion say 'hello'
Just so many truths of an absurd nature

2. **Trapped in the Bell Jar (found poem)**

Trapped in a Bell jar of seamless opportunities,
snorting lines in a velvet underground.

I sing this song of (my) self,
as the tyger burns bright in the night.
As Queen Vashti mocks Kali,
Jesus shoots up cruising,
and Vishnu lies in a catatonic stupor.
You're hunting Helene,
to take away the pain.

Your body I crave. Angel headed hipsters
lost in Bohemian Rhapsodies...
Ghosts of love rapping upon the door,
slamming poetry, across the night's
Plutonian shore.
I pay my pennies
to the boatman.

Welcome to the country town-where
Molly and Ice and Smack are cheaper
than an average feed for an average family.

Buzzing phones, life just ain't worth-living,
'less it's played out in 140 characters
for all the peasants and sycophants to read.
If religion's the opiate of the people,
then what the fuck is fame?
I'm just a poor boy
trapped inside this mediocrity.
How does a poet belong?
How does a poet survive?
Dada, dada, papa, mama, dada,
papa, mama.

Mutter, vater und herr teufel.
Mutha-fucker. Lord and Devil.
Infantile scribbling on the page,
concrete poems and suicidal linguists.
Lingua-franca bubble and squeak.

Lost in the wasteland of megabytes and kilobytes and fish and chips
wading through the multiversal slipstream
zero one zero one zero one—0101010010101010...

Binary metaphysics
the dogma of narcissistic masturbation.
Burning Rilke's promises.

Cave. Cave. Facta hominum formidolsa junt.
Veritatem quae eventa est. Duex in machine
captus est.

Buzzing noises. Desires beget desire.
Blood lust on the rise. The dawn does not quench it,
nor does it bleach it.
What's the difference between cock and cunt?
Bukowski's in the asylum,
Burroughs arrested again, added to the list of sex offenders,
Blake's sedated to his eye balls.
Poe's – he original Emo-goth.

Emily Dickinson self-harms-and posts poems on deviantart.com;
self-expression for the sake of self-expression.
My life's a work of art – the body a masterpiece,
the mind polluted, soul decayed,
everything's lost in the translation.

Published GORE Journal RMIT Volume 4. 2014.

3. *Recruit School*

He's roaring at me again.
Trembling I am. I can feel the looks
from all the other men, burning into me,
"you fucken muppet. Can't you do anything right?"

On the ground in front of me is my best friend...
My rifle. My Steyer. The spring flopping around in the dirt
the receiver group wrong way up again.

"Recruit Numbnuts...of course it would be you"
In the Reserves I was a private—here I am just a Recruit.
Primary school, high school all over again...
The bastions of masculinity,
the warrior-caste, the footballers,
'the jocks'—all off in their own segregated
groups. Only one woman in this platoon at the beginning
of our training—our internment?

She was moved on before the end of two weeks.
Too many of the men hovering in the lines at 12 am,
when she's allowed to shower. Putting temptation
out of the way—so transfer her—their excuse
We have gunners, and infantry, bombardiers
and artillery men—what the fuck she gonna do?

She had a soft kind face. Soon she would lose
the sunny disposition and become too much like
a man, too barren and fruitless to be called a woman.

Lying in my bunk at night,
wondering when the beatings will start,
wondering when they'll call a Code Red...

Every day the same—every move I make,
I will always lose this game. Silent weeping from the bunks
on the other side of the room. Top bunk shaking too fast,
he's furiously masturbating again. Maybe that's what
I'm doing here—pretending I belong.

Bottom sheet across
my right shoulder.
Morning routine—all standing at attention
before we shit, shave and shower.

Too much eczema under my chin,
on my throat—bleeding every God-damn day. Stress and the heat
of the NSW hinter-valley.

Lying in the prone position, on the range,
test and adjust—close my eyes, focus on my breathing
in and out, in and out—just listen to the beating
heart—close the world off—I am at one with the rifle,
I am at one with what I have to do.

Open my eyes and look down the small optical sight
on the handle—5 mmx zoom. Trust yourself...tune it out all
trust yourself, squeeze it gently like the wheel on a lighter;
softly—softly. Shallow thunder cracks of the firing guns.
Repeating over and over again.

Another one's roaring at me now,
Just passed my safety and rifle theory test.
95 percentile. Top one in my squad,
in the top five of the platoon.

"What ya blow him to get that score did ya?"
"NnnnnannnO..." Fuck I'm stuttering again. My eternal weakness
what they all notice right away...How much of a fraud I am
my statstatstammering--how I betray my condition

my disability every time, nerves burn through my veins.
"Bull shit. Pay to get it did ya spaz boy? You ain't smart
enough to get that score"

I'm shaking all over.
All I wanna do is put my hands to his throat
and rip out his larynx. I reckon I can do it.
His fucking laughter. His fucking condescension.

Does he want me to react?
Do I just take it....do I call him a cunt,
and put up with the charge and the incarceration?
"Numbnuts don't you have any heart...Don't you care
What I'm saying to you...you piece of shit?"

4. *Internet @ 4 am*

Blips. Digits. Scrambling like magic
across the screen. Insular cortex zombified
a spaced out Junkie on the sofa. Surrounded by
decomposing Big Mac's—new forms of life
evolving daily. Magic buttons. Digitized world.

4 AM—am I the only one awake?
light another smoke. Just ran out of green.
empty picks, bent blades and diabetic masturbation
thoughts of the hollow skin. Hollow heart.

How did I get on this website?

Who really fucking cares now anyway?
two Romanian women in various stages
of undress in front of me. One protesting that
she's actually Bulgarian, the other looks right through
me with eyes as dark as the Baltic. They tell me to strip.
Want to see what I look like, without hiding anything.
type the numbers on the screen.
they have my life—my manhood at their disposal.

It's not their slutty chat that draws you in...
it's always the casualness. The matter of fact way
they want you to stand up—want to see all of me.
Pride in my right hand. Who's the one exposed?
who's actually doing the buying and selling.

It's almost time to go. They link me into another website...
followed by another. $25. $35. $50. Am I Captain Ahab?
What is my unicorn? I know they don't really like me...
The Euro has dropped a bit. I'm paying in Australian—it's lunch time
over there. Facebook alerts me—an old flame now perpetually engaged
just poked. That's her signal—he's away tonight.

5 hour drive. But she's playing that game again. She pokes. I prod.
She pushes. I pressure. Silence. Drink more Gin.

Gotta get up for work in three hours.
another rush slowly begins to build within me.
I look at the time. The words pour out like a gushing wound.

Almost out of cigarettes. Small price to pay I guess.
Tracey is lonely.
Donna is sad.
Mark can't believe his team lost again.
Damien is waiting to hear back from a publisher
and I post a link of Nine Inch Nails.

Bone orchard poetry (website) 2013.

5. Feud.

Two men stand
heaving. Breathing.
bloodied and tired.

Train coming down the line…
gun on the platform.
Look of desperation.
Who'll move first?
Who will fall?

people hiding
behind trash cans
and pillars. News-stands
covered in the blood of
innocent passers-by.

Rumbling train
getting closer
deafened into the distance
by the heart beats of these two men.

Friends all their lives
blood feud—fuelled by
their father's greed and pride.

Gold crucifixes
and family heirlooms
hang around their swarthy necks.

Ground vibrates underfoot.
the dive for the gun in the panic
of the departing passengers.

Shots ring out. *They both fall.*

(Bone Orchard Poetry (website) 2014

6. Edge of Tomorrow

Summer days, at the edge of tomorrow,
the blanket pretends, we share no sorrow.
echoing rain falls softly on my face.
Time forgets, but never forgives,
so we always know our place.
Listen to the wind
falling through the trees
ancient songs, fading fast.

Chain saw fells another
wise old man. Sound it makes
as it falls—the gargling death
of reality—ever getting closer.
Exhaust fumes
fibre optic cable
suffocating all of us.
but do we care at all?

Wailing child,
never lets the house
sleep. The product of
the world he's found.
Wisdom beyond his years.
Edge of tomorrow
wraps itself around
our imagination.
The holy and the meek
publicly belittled, faces
of sainthood cracked.
Devotion just means
perversion. Love is just addiction.

tomorrow when the begins
whose side will you be on?
tomorrow when the world
bleeds no more—what will you
believe when death falls upon us?

7. For the 800 found in Galway

How many crimes?
how many times,
can we turn our back?
Look the other way,
day after day.
Don't speak no evil,
don't hear no truths
just live the lies
they feed you.

What makes a servant of God?
turn from the path?
What makes power corrupt?
So convincingly?

Innocent lives condemned
by the absoluteness of bureaucracy
How many crimes?
Just how many lies are hidden
by the collar and the habit?
The yarmulke or the turban?

How many lies,
how many times
must the steeple
and the tabernacle
conceal horrors
of the virtuous and holy,
purity of white
only shrouds black of heart,
for just so long...

8. I...

I—is not a concept, I can easily recognise.
Who sees themselves as an I, and not a Me?

I—that pronoun so powerful, so triumphant,
that Monarchs the world over, seldom use,
to denote themselves. Kings and Queens have no
concept of self. They're always US or WE.

Even Shakespeare is loathed to use it,
as much as us. *Methinks. Thine. Thy. Thou. Thee.*

Beautiful cadences, soft and subtle, supple
off the tongue. So poetic, so dramatic.

Seem so much clearer than the accusatory "YOU";
or the demonstrative "I"
...I believe this. I want that.
I must have you.

Tell me what do you hear first, in those two little sentences.
That both bring about good and evil, hope and calamity.
I love you.
I hate you.

But I—I—do now wonder if I can truly
conceive of myself as myself; and not I,
or me. The concept I ever truly
have of myself existing, is when I see
a photograph, or an Instagram,
or my reflection in the mirror.

My eyes are lenses.
My eyes capture all the light;
vantage point, close up, aspect,
shot and frame. But am I really seeing
anything at all?

And not just perceptions,
of what I think I see?
There it is again, repeated twice,
in a short little line. Dominant,
triumphant—capitalised.
Not the world of all you need is love...
All we are saying, give peace a chance?
No! Not for a long time.

Now it's I want it all. I want it now. Me. Me. Me. Me. I want. I need!

9. Paper Moon

Paper moon
broken chair.
lost riddles
drowning in the ocean
of people. Concrete jungle
bright burning lights.

Are stars nothing more
than minute pinholes
in the curtain of night?

Too many people zipping by me,
it's like I'm a camera
filming the world
When people talk to me
Are they are breaking the fourth wall?

Terrified of intimacy
but craving human touch,
like walking, talking wax work,
too scared when you embrace

I will crumble. I will melt.
sensory overload
is not just lights and sounds
emotions—to me it's all
like a bathroom tap—
it's either on full blast,
not knowing when to stop.

Or it drips, drips, drips
until it fades away.

Paper moon
rainbow world.
Look through the prism
spectrums and waves
what do you see?

I am nothing but
a robot of skin
and flesh and blood,
sensory processing
unit's failing...

Numbers and words
don't exist to me,
how do I do what I do
when I just put them on the page,
hoping it sounds right.

If my brain doesn't understand
patterns work why don't I dress in plaid?
how can I take the time

all those pretty words,
and make perfect rhymes?
just my luck an untreatable curse.

10. Are We Not?

In the mind you are free
floating in the imagination
you are always free.

No matter what they say,
you can be a butterfly,
even if you don't have wings.

I am a refugee from the status quo,
Poetry is my promised land.

My homeland lost decades ago,
patch of dirt with a Shell sign on top
of it now.

In my mind, we are all free
from these corporeal forms,
we are dancing on the water,
like dust upon the dawn,
our genders, our race,
our identities floating
away from all constraints.

Who is the world,
to tell us who to love?
Brother to brother?
sister to sister?

Are we not all one and the same?
Are we not all beautiful and ugly?
Are we not all not martyrs—
Are we not all selfish and proud
jealous and loyal?

Freedom rides upon the horizon,
am I not the black man and the white woman?
are you not Asian and Arab?

Every Jew has the same blood as a Catholic...
Are we not the same,
for love is all we seek?

11. Words

Time slides out of view,
when I'm lying next to you.
Clouds fall upon the dawn.
Sky might fall tonight,
but being here with you,
I know I shall be re-born.

Too many words in our language
too many phrases, too many deceits.

Too many wasted words—for commercials
and for cinematic television events—
where have the words of love now gone?

How can that little word,
that means so much be wasted
by all of us; for a song, for a meal,
for a glass of wine, a football team,
the latest celebrity craze.

That word that rolls off the tongue.
Teeth and tongue and mouth collide,
as I say I love you. As I pledge my devotion.
But have I gone too far?

Have I said too much?
pushed the envelope too far now?
As we embrace before another dawn,
you leave before the morning...

12. What Are Poets Good For?

The dead are piling up outside my window.
Hot burning sun melts the flesh.
Hope rots faster than skin.
Will I be measured at the end,
by all of my mistakes, my deadly sins?

Or, will I be mounted on the wall
of mediocrity? Critics and rivals,
friends and readers mourning
my premature demise?

Seven deadly deeds of perpetual
love drain from me adolescent poetry
and the fallacy of fleeting fame.
Neurotic poetry
and self-indulgent art—is
that all we're good for now?

Making women cry
and lost lonely goths
feel at home. Masturbating
on this page. Psychological
self-harming more socially
acceptable than a man crying in public.
Can't kick a ball or shoot a gun,
gotta be a fag.

No man speaks
that softly. Nothing lasts
more than we allow it to.

Internet makes us all
think we're Picaso,
Dali or Edgar Allen Poe,

but really deep down
we're just all Van Gough
sans the talent or the insight.

13. Often.

Often....often you make me feel so alive.
Often. Often—you make me feel that I don't
exist at all.

I often wish you would hate me.
I often wish you would find someone else,
let me be alone and back to my happy/miserable
life.

And not feel stuck in this miserable/happy life;
we're the one you love is splayed out before you
but has fallen asleep from the long shift at work,
the stress of her life. Or because she's scored
and is high again. Lying in the bed, or the on the bed
or on top of me. Often—often, I let temptation
get the best of me. And dream. That we are the same
but just so slightly different. But, then there are the days
where we hardly talk.

Our shared existence
our experience just a half forgotten note,
in the scrapbook of mediocrity.
Often, often....often, often—I reach out
in the night, like the old days and remember
that you didn't stay the night, like I used...

Often, often...

14. Lost In The Days Of Endless Night

Sunlight's dancing across
the horizon—pink scarred sky,
purple tide coming in tonight.
She was the dawn,
I was the dusk.

One morning I woke
to find myself,
lying with our bodies
sacred, entwined
in her bed.

She was the shadow,
dancing in the corners
of the darkness, in my dread,
in my dread—she saved me.
Forever living, the days
of endless nights.

I watch the sorrow
in your eye,
forever drifting into the past,
no thoughts of tomorrow.

I see your face in the morning sky;
my heart's forever with you.
Trapped in our days,
of endless night.

Touch of flesh
upon flesh, my only
nourishment.

Only truth, worth knowing
is the taste of her lips
upon mine.

We danced upon the darkness.
We devoured all the misery
of the world. Don't you dare
forget—that feeling.

Absent from reality,

trapped in the days
of endless nights.

Frozen by her smile.
As we slide in and out
of each other's consciousness.

Even the slightest touch,
sends lightning through all of my being.

Lay your hands upon my heart,
lay your body in my hands.
Lost in that maze again
lost in the days of endless nights.

Put your mind at ease.
Shut the gate, make sure the
Dog doesn't get out.

Standing in your doorway;
never felt so alive.

We embrace,
almost a lifetime
separated, yet always
almost meeting again.

We stole each other's lives,
we devoured all of our suffering;
lived that night, that every stranger
every friend—needs, those days
of endless nights.

Why can't I breathe,
unless I see you?
Why can't I sleep,
unless we've spoken?

Drunk too much
from the fountains of bliss your kiss;
and here we are again,
here we are again...

Lost in the days of endless night.

15. Auguries Of The Non-Conforming/Conformist.

Slouching towards nirvana,
benedict and solemn in my approach
to oblivion. I blew the back of the head
off a man who walked across my shadow on the side-walk.
I dressed the corpse in the headlines of Celebrity and fame.

You're rolling us a joint, I'm composing
ill-fated rhymes. Soul decays body entwines—
into the abyss of *'could have been better'* if he
just applied. The day yawns, at the seldom delivering night.

All of us—staccato marching, in this Zombie zeitgeist
giant fob watch, watching all of us—clock strikes
deep fryers, icing sugar, meat by-products
and petroleum—the healthiest diet of the masses.

Masturbating over the on-coming destruction
of all things. Take a seat at the bar, Charon informs me,
my check's bounce—all my plastic's rejected. Fraudulent poets;

God-like actors, Herculean footballers, Drug—addled prophets
lost in their own brown paper bags of despair and lunatic
ramblings. Bunch of us about to leave soon. Two big coins
in my pocket—eye lash dust upon the faded letters of the coins.

What am I? who are you? What are we? Why are naked and bound
together in the fifth circle of Hell?
Wanna-bes, and losers, weaklings
never-weres face the world with a loaded gun.

Skull-fucking the brains out with hot lead; for anyone who
they assume is disrespecting them.
Real men don't waste their time on women
and a world who aren't interested in them.

We create and destroy our worlds—with stroke of the pen
or brush. So—from my liver and my lungs, inside out,
will I rot? Is martyrdom calling for you my dear beloved,
on the needle crucifying yourself—just something to do
to pass the time? When will puritans and the non-believers
finally get the hint—G-d simply just doesn't give a shit.
Once the game's in motion, the die is cast, the curtains

have raised and all the players are on stage—the author
cannot and should not be called upon to explain.

G-d blew his brains out in the back of a pink Cadillac
Burroughs and Rilke dared him their souls; that he didn't have the balls.

Shakespeare now works
for Days of Our Lives and Mozart's writing jingles
for Coca-Cola and the Disney corporation.

Everyone dreams of virtual reality,
the perfect arse and the perfect smile,
ultra white teeth and a vegan diet—can't
let any of the poor animals suffer this week.

Next week I'm starting the Atkins diet,
and will start reading L. Ron Hubbard again,
maybe if I publish more poems, I'll be an attractive
candidate this time.

16. Forgotten Wars

Legend and myth,
fuelled by the arrogance,
the ignorance of the British Bulldog.
Sneak attack in the Dardanelles.
Blunder of the century.

Passchendaele and the Somme
blood soaked poppy fields,
unknown soldiers, buried
en masse.

Forged in fire
and blood. Forgotten
stories. A day glorifying
death or blood?

Yet, sometimes those old Clichés
are full of truths.

To the victor goes the spoils.
History written by the winners,
loser are succumbed to the catalogue cards
in an old dusty library.

Cenotaphs on bronze and majestic,
religious icons in a secular age,
don't tell the story of the blood
soaked dirt, the statues were
erected on.

Forgotten language
disappeared customs,
dispersed—people;
silent song lines
Gypsies are forgotten
so are the infirmed
and the artistic; in the tomes
of the holocaust. Armenians
denied on the shores of Gallipoli.

Forgotten wars,
unhealed wounds,
Forgotten victims
of state wide crimes.

Forgotten Heroes,
well-fought causes,
Freedom of speech,

Gay marriage,
the right to vote.
Forgotten wars,
unhealed wounds,
Forgotten victims
of state wide crimes.

Forgotten stories
faded memories.
Forgotten wars,
leaves a bitter taste
in the mouth.

War crimes at least
resolve the rumours
with evidence and
investigations...

Massacres and genocide
swept under the black arm
band of history—scapegoat
of all manner of horrors...

17. Hell Is Other People.

Hell is other people.
Misery is love.
Solitude is heaven.

Salvation—a night full of strangers,
no possibility of future interactions.
No possibility of ever acknowledging
each other passing each other on the street.

Hope is a prison—that only the foolish
condemn themselves to.
Does she really live on love street?
In her eyes—am I just another fresh piece of meat?

Hell is other people.
Misery is love.
Solitude is heaven.

Bourbon dulls the senses,
and cigarettes only remind me
of your kiss.

Raining all night again,
the night's found an expression
for my frustration...
Hell is other people.

18. 800 Angels

Shedding light on the past,
always reveals the shadows.
Skeletons of shame,
crimes of desperation and pain.
800 angels, still haven't found
their wings.

How can they be called brides of Christ?
When daughters of Herod seem, much
more precise?
Burying the past,
only leaves the future
with a bitter, rotten taste
in the mouth.
Never-ending questions,
disgust and award silences.

What answers given
to frantic, desperate,
ashamed mothers, longer
pure—never had the chance
to be called a bride.

Too much fun, too much time
for the wilder things in life.
How is this morality
when throughout most
human history, marriage
is another word for bondage
or female-slavery?

What did they die of?
small pox? Famine, or just neglect?
they found them in the septic tank...
not buried, not cremated to hide the crime.

Just cast out—put out of sight, out of mind.
Institutional blindness
the eighth deadly sin,
that was never passed down
to priests, or nuns, kith or kin.

19. The Idea.

Pink Galahs take to flight
smudging wintry skies.
Old brown shoes wrapped around
telephone lines—hidden from G-d's view,
can we truly start behaving the way
we long to?

Words are my actions,
actions are my thoughts.
Am I both of the body
and of the soul?
Does the mind forces
its will upon the senses,
emotions have no control?

Falling into the world of
tannoy promises
and transistor prayers.
World cup's about to start.
My TV is unplugged on principle.

Hollow Goddesses scroll across my screen,
semi-naked and winking; every desire
in the palm of my hand.

Are adjectives for the poet,
like flab and extra kilos for the boxer?
Every punch—every bout, every knock out
every win, loss or draw, forever getting
closer and closer to the pure unmistakable
image—the perfect sentence, the perfect line.
The most direct communication of the idea?

20. Stranger's Remorse

I watched as he lay dying before my eyes.
Skin under my finger nails,
blood curdling cry.
Yet, no sirens do I hear,
no threat of conviction or gaol.

No explanations. No rhyme no reason.
He was just in my way,
as I walked across the street.
Trying to light a cigarette
in the heavy wind and pelting rain.

All I remember was
his shadow on the pavement,
under the blinking,
broken street light.
Don't even remember how
we started the fight.

All I can see in my mind—
is him falling to the ground,
my hands, my shirt,
my face awash in blood and muck.

It wasn't how I expected it to be.
Rich, dark red, a crimson sea.
Don't even know his name,
or how he came to be,
on the street at that
exact time on that exact night...

He'd have a family or some mates,
he'd have someone that would
care for him, somewhere, somehow...

Light another cigarette,
open the door to my empty flat,
the guilt of my crime,
the emptiness mocking me...

His ashen face, his grey cold eyes,
his blackening tongue—within moments
I saw his light diffuse and retreat...
What was the mist I saw dancing into
the Aether of night...pour another whiskey,
praying that by the time I end the bottle,
I've forgotten all about him

But I know that ain't gonna happen.

21. (Leave) All Of Us?

Standing on the corner,
thumb out to the highway,
beautiful girls washed out
by the mushroom clouds of neon lights.

Whispered love, floats upon a leaf.
Tomorrow's joy foreshadowed by today's sorrow.
Rendezvous', elegant encounters seem so long, but are oh so brief.

Dreamscapes and activist Zebras, purple elephants.
Yesterday sneaks in the backdoor, just before dawn,
shoes in one hand—bag of full of wasted dreams in the other,
on tiptoe, creaking floor, mum and dad's door a jar.
How sad would they be if they knew
how she strayed, how long and how far?

What is this talk of me and you?
What is the promise of tomorrow?
Vodka at 5:10 in the morning,
melted ice and flat tonic water.
Has to be a metaphor somewhere there?

Why am I finally looking at other options,
while you seem to be drawn closer and
closer towards me?

G-d has a cruel sense of fairness.
G-d doesn't want anyone to get together,
In the Torah he is jealous and vain,
in the parables of Christ, he is fair
and subdued...When did G-d enter rehab?

and when did G-d leave

All of us...?

22. Remembrance Day 2013
(Armistice)
(For my granfather Ernie)

Photographs fade,
memories remain.
Lost men—forgotten
their legend lives on.
Woman alone in the country.
Her two year old son playing on the floor,
shawl over her infant daughter,
nursing at her breast.

Every creaking
wind, and snapping twig,
makes her think today the Priest
will come. Or the postman.
Or worse, his mother.

Baked dry soil
dead trees and sparse
vegetation. So different from the Somme,
the mud, the slush, the blood.
The mustard.
The coffee table in the drawing room
over flows with maps and letters he's sent
from the front.

Postcards, souvenirs—if they
were upper-class he would have been on
the grand tour—not living like a Moll in that never
ending Hell. Dust and yellow smoke.

Muck and worms invade fresh made wounds.
Officer's Whistle seem so childish, so
out of place at the end of every skirmish.
The sun doesn't shine here.

Even on clear days, no rain,
no clouds, the sun just will not shine.
Disgusted at the whole affair.

Knock on the door, wakes her
from her tortured dreams of mutant men,
faces, legs, arms torn, worn, blown away.

The black robes. The white collar.
She opens the door, O'Malley in his usual way
disarming grin, "Better put the kettle on".

Her son drops a porcelain cup,
it shatters on the hardwood floor,
her legs give in, she crumbles into
the priest's arms. Her heart
in dozen tiny pieces all over the hardwood floor,
no blood, no mess.

Shellshock! Shellshock!
Shellshock! Shellshock!

The reverberation of the cup smashing,
artillery and carbines, lightning when
there is no storm. Thunder when there are
no clouds. She doesn't say a word.

She can't even bury him.
She takes a breath and moves to her child,\

"What have you done now?"
she says in that casual way mothers do.
scoops up the shattered cup
places it into the hearth of the fireplace.

Husband's face is starring at her, smiling at her
with his eyes like he used to. All those photographs, all those images,
all those reminders...his glaring smile mocking her.
What am I supposed to do now? With Ernie and Cath?
What happens now?

She bundles up all of the letters, the photographs,
their wedding album, all of it for the fireplace.

She watches the flames dance around the boiling,
bubbling photographs, her heart hardens.
Her soul quietly shouting. She turns around and fixes her
hair in the hall mirror.

Agnes from next door is on the porch...
"Hello Agnes fancy a cuppa?"

23. Auguries of Virtual Reality

Lying in the palms of the world,
she's walking through the rainclouds,
moonbeams and ghost rainbow faeries,
circling around her long raven hair...
In her eyes—the night unfurls,
dark birds, cawing, resting on ancient boughs,
painted—unfinished sky becomes our Plutonian prairie

No-one else breathes in this palace of the night,
we lie in the arms of bliss—forgotten all worldly cares.

Time is fleeting—
experience loses all its meaning
when innocence fails to inspire,
the pure of heart.

All of us are guilty
Waiting for the miracle
to start.
Silence creeps into the mind
comfortably numb from the elixir
of anxiety. In narrow streets will
I find my home?

Why does comfort breed contempt?
Black Queen in the lungs of industry
marches us all to our death—white
Queen seduces martyrs to sacrificial rites,
prime-time pornography
Sweat-shop reality—better phone better lifestyle.

The vampiric embrace of celebrity
Facebook infamy—Instagram
sexting—anal sex on first dates
in the 8th grade—and the Ogres
of conformity anguishing in the cloisters
of the temple of modernity.

Time's ticking away
faster than we can breathe
in and out—in and out. Life—constantly decaying,
the world is glutton—and we are all just zombies,
gorging on the last remains of humanity...

24. Almost six in the morning

Almost six in the morning,
it's almost dawn. Words are refusing to form.
Patience running low, and the other side of me
starting to stir.
I get a good line and then delete from
my memory, before I can even work out the rhyme.
Almost six in the morning, and I'm labouring the point
because I can't think of anything to say.
Dogs are barking
in the street, internet porn holds little interest to me these days.
Running low on cigarettes
and it's too fucking cold
to run down the hall half naked
for another shot of vodka.
It's just gone six.
Morning Television best known cure for insomnia.
inane banter—happy-happy talk.

Middle-aged men surrounded by blondes
all under forty, yet all creeping ever closer, closer to that first nail
in the coffin of their on-screen career.

Banality is pouring through my fingertips,
sitting up in my bed tapping out verses,
like an organ grinding monkey on display.

25. Silent Girl

Silent girl's voice
deafened by the noise
of the world.

Burning tears,
hidden scars,
buried from the world,

Demon hands
the body remembers
every touch of water
of flesh. Of sunlight
of the breeze,
the body always remembers.

Whispered words
filled with dread,
"our little secret.
No-one will ever understand".

Silent girl
cuts again tonight.
Every part sullied
has to burn, has to be carved.

Another hit quiets the world,
another dose brings her closer
to serene mist.

Medicated bliss
secrets hidden in plain sight.

Silent girl
longs for the day,
yet, always craves the night.

Silent girl
knows that nothing
will ever silence the dreams,
dull the memories.

Silent girl
longs for the end
but knows the pain it will bring.
Not to her, but everyone
that doesn't understand.

Silent girl loves the world,
but fears the future.

Silent girl
reveals all
too she trusts the most,
he uses like a blunt knife,
threatens to ruin her life,
just so she will hate him,
like he hates himself.

Silent girl
with the forgiving heart,
can only go so far,
before the breaking point's reached.

Silent girl
Forgives all
but never forgets.

26. ***Hours***

Hours go by in an empty room,
hours filled with empty promises—devoid
of contact, sights, scents and sounds of
normality. Absent from the average coming
and going of your daily life.
You do what you gotta do to keep on going.

Adults playing childish games,
games in the hallway.

'Fuck off' "fingers crossed. I'm barley".

Some self-harm. Some fight. Some give up.
Some yell night and day. Some kick and scream.
I smoke cigarettes and dream.

Some pray to G-d, to release them from this reality.
Some listen to the voices—the demons
in their head. And they let the voices,
lead them astray. I'm still writing rhymes
to keep insanity at bay. Can you tell me
again what were my crimes?

27. Tell Me

Tell me about the emptiness in noise.
tell me all about the sound that swallows
the silence, when we clap our hands.
What comes first?

When do our lips
actually touch, our breath
our tongues
become one, in a lover's kiss?
What comes first the thought
or the action? The word
or the breath?

Is the breath of eternity
the breath, the whoosh
the rolling, roaring
of the tumultuous ocean?
Melodic and robust,
perfect in form.

Function becoming distraught
discordant on the rocks.
So, tell me all about
how God and Love
can't exist? Tell me
without dogma
or ideology, personal
pronouns or personal attacks...

Conventional constraints.

Tell me if or when
love will begin?

Tell me all about the next world.
Tell me all about my frailties
my failures and my triumphants

Tell me what happens if
from this precipice I jump?

28. Touch Of Blade

The touch of the blade
upon naked flesh
suicide is not the act
of isolation.
You are never alone
when the moment comes.
Shadows linger
the demon whispers
and pushes you forward.

Voices in your head
tie the knot.
Place the chair
under the roof beam.
Demon loads the shot gun.

The shadows seal the hose
with tape, from the exhaust pipe
to the driver's side window
shadow king makes sure
the garage door is firmly closed.

29. ***Bird Song***

How does a bird know it's a bird?
is it only ever singing its own name?
a proclamation of the self—upon the dawn
upon the leaves of the tree,
to be carried by the wind?

Or does the bird sing
because it has to,
to survive?
laughing Kookaburras
warbling Magpies
caw-cawing Crows.
Yawning Owls
and stalking Hawks
far, far up in the sky...

Do birds sing to the glory of G-d?
Or just because the sun is out?
Do they sing to attract a mate?
warn off predators—or do they
sing just because the Poet
writes poetry and the painter
paints?

30. Why Do I love?

How do I love you?
when you leave me
with the horrors of my mind?
Why do I love you
when so many times
you cast me aside?

Why are you in my life,
when half the time I hate you?
Why do we often sleep side by side,
when so often I regret even knowing
you?

Why do I wish tonight
after you leave my side,
that we had never entered each other's
lives?

31. ***Free-form***

Free form
Floating words

lost appointment

Last anointment
Prophet lackadaisical

Promises. Boundaries
Pushing.
Conformity
nothing original.
Window dressing
Screaming the loudest
Saying nothing at all.
No more truths
Just old lies
re-packaged.

Dogma changes
corruption remains the same.

Truth what is it? Where did it go?

Truth is I hate you.
truth is I love you.
Truth is I need you.
truth is leading us away
from love.
What is the answer? What is truth.

Formless. Free.
Floating words on the horizon

Prettier the box,
the more tempting
Pandora finds it....
What is truth?

32. Nocturne

1.

We sit in a drawing room,
Chopin's Nocturnes are
strolling through our minds.

We sit in antiquated chairs,
drinking an old man's summer wine
talking of Platonic ideals of Form
and Pythagorean concepts of time.

I can see the old Gum trees.
and the old world ornamentals.
twinkling in the deep red sky.

But that was too long ago
to think upon now.
Time has moved, so have we.
Some of us married. Some of us engaged,
some with more kids, with new kids,
and some hope to have one on the way.

And, we all live in longing
for those days again, those days
when all was possible through
art and music, and idealism,
where wine, woman and song
could deliver us from any disharmony.

But, our masters have been
resigned to the fate of mediocrity
vanquished by their own principles,
the devotees and the wanna-bes,
leaderless, direction poor,
is there hope for the old, old ways,
does anyone care at all now, about
the metaphysical and sensual,
our brains fatty with luxuries
that the true artist can ill-afford.

2.

What lies between the act
and the fall?

Blakeian mysteries
taunt me in my waking
dreams. The fool and the wise man
see not the same tree—is the difference

between the prophet, the madman
or the charlatan? Just the quality
of the followers or the amount
of followers you have?

Because I do not hope
to dare fall in love again
because I dare not live
stuck in this malignant game,
because you are running now,
running from every possible
outcome. Each and every chance
of pain.

3.

Night rolled out before us,
we walked along beach,
arms around each other,
your dog metres out in front,
the last throes of light,
shining out from behind the clouds,
seems like such a distant memory,
since we lay in each other's arms,
contemplating what life would
truly be like alone—not with
each other—not with any other
just alone.

But, you talk of the jasmine in the air,
and the roar and whoosh of the evening tide,
the descending hands of time, forever
stalking our enchantment and our joys.

Red skies. Red eyes
Knife of time denies us
all our victories, no matter
how small.

The Art of Being of Human (2013)

33. Earth Born Child
(Inspired by Kain White)

Earth born child,
weeps into life.
Dawn of time
soon shall rise,
the thought of life
comes before the action,
the word and after the breath.
The world dies
every night,
the sun gives birth
daily.

Earth born child
screams in the night,
all the world burning with strife.
The wailing child
and the dying man
share an intimacy
we all soon forget.

Wisdom of infancy
is corrupted by maturity;
the hope of salvation
is lost in the oceans
of our vanity.
Lingering shadow mourns
sunlight. The womb of life
holds us all together
mother moon
and father sun.

Earth born child
lost in the forever
in the echo of the wilds;
Earth born child takes a life,
gives solace to the night.
Are we not all animals?
Are we not all creatures of the wild?
Between the shadow and the mask
belies our own twisted reality... (for colab 2014/bendarts 2014)

34. Autumn in the City

We sit under Chloe's watchful gaze,
it's a freezing night, but all we can
feel, the heat emanating from our touch.
We can pass hours in here without speaking,
we just sit and watch the world pass by us.
The burnt orange of Flinder's street's shrouded
in a reddish hue. Rain's teaming down now.

Day of dodging traffic and the rain, jumping on and off
trams and trains whenever we see the Stasi in track pants.
In the afternoon, gorging ourselves on dumplings,
in Tattersall's lane.

Getting lost in the labyrinth of the gallery
by the south bank of the river. Gustave Dore
is haunting us. You tell me 'focus on the red.

Close your eyes and think about the red';
I do as you inspire and the burning
red dances all around me.

Little Red Riding Hood, seduced by the big
bad wolf.

Clanging trams and clopping horses,
rain's stopped for a few moments
and we dash under newspapers
under the arches of the old town hall.
We embrace as we hide away
we kiss with fire. Steam rises from
our bodies.

35. Slogan

"No Fracking in National Parks. " Solar panels are ugly".
"No hunting in National parks. End the massacre of native water birds"
"Don't want them over here, taking our jobs. Poisoning your way of life"
"Resources stretched too far. "Wind turbines making my kids sick"
"Coal seam mining creates toxic air. Kills the pristine environment".
"Don't mine the Kimberly". "Mining creates job, closes the gaps. It's better
for indigenous communities".

"STOP THE BOATS!" Our greatest moral challenge".
"End the slaughter of innocent Cattle". "Stop the Gulag battery farms".
White noise drowns out the world.
White noise. White noise.
Mobile phone towers and satellite dishes.
Books just mementos of Grand Pa's day, walking five miles
in the sleet and rain in an old dogged pair of un-cobbled shoes.

White noise—blurred lines.
"Refugees welcome". "NO taxation without representation".
"A new way". "A stronger Australia". "Stop the boats".
"Cut the smugglers". "A positive society".

"Change the lies". "Buy back the boats", "Fair on boats"
"Save the Whales".

"Save the Rainforests"
"Milk is murder"
"Pedo lives here!"
Surely the mean a Paedophile,
not someone with a foot fetish.
"Milking a cow is tantamount to gang rape".
"Don't eat me"
"Smoking Kills"
"Buy Australian Made".

"If you drink and drive, you're a bloody idiot"
"Jesus heals all—Abortions kill children".
"Woman's body. Woman's right...
"Governments change, lies remain
the same".
"Not in my name".
"Take back the night".

36. Rural Life

1. Februum

February crawls out of you, like a habit,
you're forever trying to break.
In the North they say, a hundred feet buried in snow.
The long white winters, the barren fields, old lonely
people trapped, buried alive in old Eastern bloc
apartments.

Portraits of Lenin or Thatcher
covered in dust. Silver Birch trees glistening
in red moon nights. On the other side
of that crooked spinning orb, the barren-ness
of life remains.

The dry dead dirt, the decaying
trees. The long dry summers, flame trees burning
across the horizon. Purple, orange and burnished
dawns.

The natural process of Eucalypt trees, bush tucker
and marsupial life cycles; that we simply do not understand.
Bush fires blaze—across three connected states;
hundreds of homes, dozens of lives lost.

We mourn the tragedy. Man's home is his castle.
Is every life truly sacred?
But—the flames are not our enemy.
Those scorching days, sweltering nights
where you can't eat or drink, sleeping's out of the question.
We have no respect for death.
We just run from it.

We just run,
run as fast as we can.
We cannot see the process
the natural wonders on display.
Maidens drabbed in purple,
dancing, gaily around the flames.

The purification of life,
of the year that's past and the year that's just begun.
Summer—winter just different hands on the clock
of fate.
The day of love and passion, burning desire,
is placed in the middle of this phase, to rekindle life,
to cut away the dead flesh of a relationship.

February is the season of death,

no matter where you are.
But, is death just the end? Or is it just us
merely walking through another door.

2. Rain Song

A thousand miles away from here,
in the opaque red centre, some kids
have never seen the rain.
Never smelt that bitter-sweetness
when it comes bucketing down.
Never felt that stillness, that pregnant
pause, at 2AM when it's too hot to sleep
and cicadas and crickets are tormenting
you at night, with their song.

But when it arrives,
nothing stops the rain.
The mud and the muck,
that washes away crops
still growing, and those
that are primed for harvest.

The endless deluge
after arid months of droughts
the torrents washing away
the life you've made.
Hell or high-water,
drought and famine.
But, nothing is cruel
and fast as the water.

Droughts and decay,
take months, years, decades.
Blink of an eye and the very ground
you're standing on,
falls, crumbles, all away...away...

But, I always wonder,
when the flood banks recede,
who tells the rain, those poor
Bastards have had enough?

But who will ever stop the rain?
Who ends the endless pain?
Who brings shelter from the storm?
What happens if the rain doesn't stop?
Is Noah out there already, putting his plans in action?

Day on the Farm

1.

Who loves a sun burnt country?
A land of corrugations, up turned V8 Commodores
splattered Roos on the highway. Shell service stations.
MacDonald's. KFC. Subway. As far as the eye can see.

One stop shops of mini, maxi, multi-corporations.
Driving a full day and half the night through
the most spectacular landscape in the world—everyone's
heads tantalized by their screens. iPads, iPhones, DVDS;
they don't see the mountains, the forests, the ship wrecked coast.
Mum asleep. Up most of the night before making lunches
for the car. Talking to her Mum in Bathurst about to go under the knife.
Dad almost didn't see the Wombat wobbling, like half solid moulded jelly
crossing the highway. Slammed on the breaks. Kids crash forward
into their screens.
"Dad what you do that for?" "Not funny Dad!"
"Everything alright love?' Mum says under closed eyes.
"Almost hit a Wombat". Oldest daughter chimes up, "Oh is it okay? Can we go see it?
That would look cool on my wall and my Tumblr".

2.
So, it's come to this? Five generations.
The well's dried up. I look at those greedy, little beady eyes.
"Mayhte...just sign on the dotted line. And you will be a very wealthy man".

What is it about city dwellers? And their stupid way of speaking.
Their condescending, patronizing way of saying, "mate" or "buddy";
using phrases and words no-one says anymore,
"Dry as dead dingo's donger"..
Jesus man., who actually says that anymore. I studied in the city you tosser.
Have three degrees in chemistry,
environmental science and agricultural management.
You bastard. I had no choice but to sell my land.

We can't compete with a corporatized town.
All our neighbours sold out years ago.

Family fed this country, two world wars, great depression.
My uncle was in parliament. You think of me as some red-neck hick.
What choice did I have?
'fake an industrial accident' like my mates had done.
Tractor or Earth mover falling on them.
Beheading/impaling or crushing themselves into a family jackpot?

Wife and kids move to the city, start again.
Multi-million dollar life insurance...what kinda man does that?
Breaks the hearts of all his loved ones, cause family pride and manhood

put into the vice of men like you. What sort of man would that make me?
To shirk my responsibilities? Pride and family name too many crosses to bear.

What will they say about me now?
How will they find me?
Will the beam break, or my neck,
before it's stretches out. Seen cows caught up
in fences and in twists of rope. Most people
don't understand how hanging works.
You don't break your neck. You don't stretch it.
You suffocate. The rope tightens,
your legs move around, almost comically in the absence
of ground. Even though you put yourself here.
The body still tries to fight it.

It still tries to fight it hard and fast.
Your body goes into shock. You void your bowels
and you almost convince yourself, that
you're gonna survive it.
Just before your last breath.

3.
The cruelty of nature, isn't cruelty at all.
The ignorance of humanity,
that becomes arrogance is true cruelty.

We have to intervene when a bird's nest
is abandoned. A dazed, confused Joey
is standing next to its mother, just ploughed down
by a truck on the Pacific highway.

But, do we know how many animals are extinct
so we can have mobile phones
and the microchip?

Auguries of wisdom—
of hope, lost in the multitude of perpetual gratification.

When was the last time you walked among the trees
that didn't have a road, a bike path
trash cans, and free Wifi with café latte?
have you ever not noticed how
long you've been walking for,
only to feel a thousand pairs of eyes.
gazing into your soul.
No-one around,
and you can barely hear singing bird,
but something keeps darting from tree to tree
its less than a blur.
Dust in the corner of your eye.
A simple life full of pleasures and distraction.

Automation is the new mythos.
 Self-perpetuating man-made dogma.

Every farm is a factory. Every factory a corporate entity.
Every corporate entity now has unalienable human rights.
Coca-cola and Nestles now
own most of South America's drinking water.
Fresh water isn't a human right, until it's caffeinated.
While the soil constantly gets saltier.

Scarred sacred trees bleeding.
Their brothers, sisters, their cosmology—
their dreaming flattened for a football oval
 and a new fruit juice processing plant.
What I wouldn't do for just the simple
pleasures of life.

37. First Dawn

Dawn's so intrusive.
Nothing worse than
being disturbed, from
that elixir, that unicorn
so elusive. You were the night

I was the light. Lost in the memories
of what we should and should
not be.
New flavours. New sensations.
New encounters. Conversation started,
never-ending. Words you whispered
upon my heart. Etched onto the pages
of my life. Venetian blinds cast strange
Dada shadows across your naked back.

I'm addicted to your heartbeat,
our bodies entwined. We devour
each other. Like a feast for a starving man.
Like a rain drop in a drought torn land.
Time has lost all meaning now. And here we are.

Your crimson lips,
blood red nails, scratching down my back,
clawing my belly.
Velvet tongue, your scent is my
intoxicant.
Your saliva—my lubricant.

I trace my hands, along the contours of your
soul. Burnt out cones, empty syringes,
smashed bottles and empty
resolutions. The wedding band, now on a chain
around your neck, hanging majestically
in the valley of your breasts, looks upon me
scornfully as you groan and move
unconsciously. Why did we feel no nerves?

As we stripped the bed. Re-made it. Symbolism lost
on both of us.

Hadn't laid our eyes upon each other,
almost half our lives. Yet, we played
perfectly in tune, to the rhythms of the night.

Why don't I feel any shame,
for sharing this bed, so many times,
a bed that was never mine to share, or see...

but became our salvation.

That first morning—that first afternoon
waking up well after 2;
Walking along a promenade.
Charcoal Chicken and greasy chips.

Seagulls true omnivores of life.
Me acting like I was in Hitch's film.
You—the wild child running down the beach.
Birds take to flight.

Night before. On stage.
Another wanky art gallery,
Talking of lost love and revenge,
Sisyphean tragedies and spiritual vampires,
rivals and colleagues,
all of them commenting on my latest
misadventure, and she's there.
Snide remarks.
Drunk allegations.

Hours later in your empty house
a house that would day become my home.
Drinking Jameson, smoking pot.
You scored another hit.
My words enflamed you.
Your body drove me forward.
My addiction never satisfied.

38. Birdman

Every night, when I sleep
I dream this creature hovers
at my bedside, it now creeps.
The birdman watches,
the birdman's silent
on the lookout for any sign of violence.
And, in my dreams it chases me
flapping wings and heart wrenching scream.
Fire bursts out of its gaping beak
and eyes as black as the night is deep.
Closing in around me, no matter
where I run, or where I hide,
the Birdman's always got me
in his eye.

Wrapped in a cocoon of self-loathing and doubt
down this corridor I run. I'm trapped. No way out.
Shadows dance around me, mocking my existence,
the creature's gaining on me; I'm running as fast as I can go,
but the black dog of despair's biting at my heels, I have such
little resistance.

And there you are my darling one, trapped in a mirror
on the wall. Your accusatory face burns me, as your eyes glimmer.
I dream that I am dreaming, yet from this Hell I cannot escape.
Every turn I make, it's still behind me, forever getting closer,
have you consigned me to this inevitable fate?
Sven foot Raven with burning eyes, and scalding breath.
Under its wing it carries a note, my certificate of death.
every door of hope is lost to me. Every room is locked.
Heart's pounding in my head, breath is running out.
Stuck in this dead end, I know it's about to take me
this messenger, this harbinger of death.

39. What Have I done?

Open my eyes,
where am I?
why are my hands covered in blood?
am I hurt? Check myself. No injuries.
throbbing headache,
smell of rancid meat
and vomit all around me.
muffled voices in the distance.
my hands are shaking.
dimly lit room. Sliver of silver flashing
in front of me.
I remember a naked woman
bloodied. Screaming.
A loud bang. Then silence.
Man's voice laughing.
Did I kill her? Or was I just watching?
Did I enjoy it? Did she deserve it?

Why did she have to die? Her ashen face haunting me.
The accusations in her eye. What's become of me?
I'm naked in my dreams, covered in the half devoured flesh
of all my enemies?

What the fuck is going on?
What the fuck am I now?

Stumbling around in this stupor
something whacks me in the head.
Puts me on my arse. I look up
it's something made of glass.
I reach out it. String connected
to a bulb. I pull the string.
Illuminated room. Flesh and blood
surrounds me.
Burnt and carved up hunks of rotting bodies.
What the fuck have I done?

40. Requiem For A Dream

An angel mourns
at the shallow grave
of fate.
Thousand burning eyes
silently judging all of us
every day and every night.
Ants crawling in and out
where blood should flow,
feels like you're being buried alive.
The sand floods the pores of the skin
each grain reminds us of all of our sins.

Am I just the empty prophet
of my own religion?
Demon lover's silent whisper
upon my naked flesh; the blade
pierces the skin. Hot white addiction
is subjugated once again.

pie jesu bemoans
the passing of time.
staying up all night,
just to have something to do.
Kyrie begins,
all solemn yet rejoicing,
what will they have
to show in my offertory procession?
If the wine is my blood,
the bread is my flesh,
are we not all one
when we consume these delights?

Too many words
wasted on too many minor
points of life. Not enough
time in lying in your arms,
sleeping all day

Thriving only at night,
my own lunar sacrifice
made redundant with
every passing of time.
Skin peels at the bone,
you've found paradise
the only place you call home,
yet I've found the vehicle of my own demise.

Sacred heart's bleeding

the virgin mother sold
her body again last night.
I dreamt I met an angel
I prayed it was my second-self,
I long to have your body
naked, sweaty broken
above me once again.
By her own admission,
by her guilt, by the needle
she was thus crucified.

Cosmic wolves
are chasing me through
the cloudless sky.
am I the joker?
are you our lady of various sorrows?
what reality awaits our tomorrow?

in your bed we cast all the demons out
but our passions led our sanity in doubt...
heart full of love, body of desire,
mind as open as consciousness
don't answer my prayers
or my phone calls,
from the beginning all things
descend continually to their end

tyranny of distance
and the burning fires
that will never cleanse our desires.

41. Constraints of Desire

Desires are constrained by the weakness
of the soul. Society tells us, those feelings are wrong,
yet they're out of our control.
Man must be strong.
Just like Gibraltar—the truth's constrained by convention
two girls walking down the street arm in arm, touchy feely,
kissey—kissey. We love same sex relationships
only if it's between two hot white chicks.
our world view is an adolescent male
wanking five times a day. Gorging himself
on violence and greasy food. Why is everything
bad, still considered gay?
Burning desires
under the skin.

Every time he walks past,
I'm on fire. I know they call it a sin. But my guard was down
he's older than me.
So—he must have seduced me.

Got me drunk, and massaged my thighs.
Yet, that deep
surrender I feel within his gaze.
That deep longing,
that fire that burns for several days. What he do
if I told him, how I felt.
Would he tell his mates,
his old man.
Would life at school just get worse?
What will they do to me in the change rooms?

power is violence
how do we empower victims
when sexual violence
is the true great weapon of mass destruction?
No matter what social media says,
or what they say on TV, I know
my old man, will beat the living
shit outta me. If I confess what
he must suspect...constraints
of convention; unspoken moral codes,

42. Glamour Girl

Hair. Make-up.
Eyes. Shape.
Image. Movement.
Cut. Magic...
Fabric. Magic.
Greta Garbo.
Helen of Troy.
Cleopatra.
Aphrodite.
Sex and sensuality.
Style, grace and mystery.
The masks we hide behind.
The clothes we wear like a second skin.
Elegance and sophistication.
In these clothes we all sparkle and shine.
Glamour—aesthetics
the be all or end all, of life?
Fashion art that's pliable
movable; public art on permanent display.

Aesthetics and fantasy.
Art and conformity.
We can be anything we want to be
All we have to do is be free with our egos.
Learn to fly on the wind...
Clothes that allure.
Fitting like a second skin.

Glamour hides the pain.
Sad memories;
Scars that no cosmetic can hide.
New clothes new identity.
Mystery and fantasy...
The world is a masquerade.
You never who's behind you...

The stronger the woman,
the more confident they appear;
the softer they are inside. Elegance
and drama, moving across a crowded room.

What is that mystery hiding behind those eyes?
Sex and sensuality.
Sex is confidence.
Sensuality is style.

Hair. Make-up.
Eyes. Shape.
Image. Movement.

Cut. Magic...

Mother of pearl
and alabaster.
Midnight sapphire,
Gentle Jazz piano...
Martinis on the balcony.

Fabric. Magic.
Greta Garbo.
Helen of Troy.
Cleopatra.
Aphrodite.
Style, grace and mystery.

Who will be the one to break the spell?
To see what's burning, glowing
down below—just under the surface... (Virgin Australia Fashion Week. Artz 2013)

43. Transhumagoria

Dada
papa
mama
lala
dada
caca
mutha
fucka.
SSSSSSSSSOWWWounnnnnd
what is a poem?
what is art?
What is sex and death
and liberation—what is mind
and hope?

Cow goes moo
scatological poetry
is still shit no matter
what way you try to dress
it up. With mundane
mediocrity iambic pentameter
and four beats in the bar.
Just because IT RHYMES
doesn't make it poetry
literary and intellectual CRIMES
seems like nothing more than Signs O
da times.
Rites of spring
burn in the season
of death.

Burning in colours
of scarlet—ultra violet—ultra violence
Sun Goddess—man in the moon masturbating
over the metaphors that I'm wasting on the page.
Cut it down. Burn adjectives.

poetry for the masses? Just as egotistical
elitist ideal as En changeant en français seulement pour l'audace de tout cela. je ne suis pas juste
masturber chroniques sur la page?

what is the voice now?
what is the throat?
puppet on a string?
or am I totally in control of these songs I sing?zingzingzingzingzing

mAR
Sheen

errrr rie
of L-A-N-G-U-A-G-E
just another dodge—post mortem poetry –post modernity
dadaadadadadadadadadadadadadadDADADADA

LALALALALA

LUVA
FIE TAR

ANGEL HEADED HIPSTERS

all lost in the hAZe
0101010101010101010101010101010
a womb and a phallus—our metaphysics
our new paradigm—just another man-made myth
of sex and stagnation—impaling and birth?
Where is the hyperlinked Christ-child now?
Heaven is just a click and download away.
all experiences up for grabs now
virtual reality—reality's virtue?

Hell is losing WiFi on the train goin thru a tunnel

trans gender
--sexual
--humanist futurist orgiastic
excesses far too heavy cost to deal with.
but where is the new divine feminie spirit?
sacred earth mother? Virgin and pure?
no such thing as a virgin on chat roulette
so many girls in the real world brainwashed
into false ideology 'gotta be a slut' or no-one
will want ya.

We have the machines
but nothing ever comes with an instruction
manual.

desires but no direction.
ability but lacking wisdom.

The shy young man, too afraid to talk
to girls at school—retreating into the world
dancing on his screens—one extreme to the next
what does it matter voyeuristic obsession.
barely legal—to Japanese incest family game
shows—guess the genitalia—what does your
mother or daughter taste like?

Your body is your living work of art?
when is it going on permanent display?
do you peel layers of skin if the critics

give you a bad review? Is this art because I say it is?
or is self-indulgent bullshit,
still self-indulgent bullshit?
if I have a message is it flawed?
or pretentious or am I just preaching,
ranting and waving?
where will this ennui lead us?
where does Transhumagoria

end?

(an experiment in automatic writing and L-A-N-G-U-A-G-E and sound poetry forms)

44. Scatter

Scatter the bones of life
across the pavement again.
Time heals
dreams repeal
the sentence of the street.

Knowing less
wanting more
the fallacy
remains the same.
dreaming today
loving tomorrow
hope is nothing more
than a lasting fall
of the leaves.

I sing a song
I make a bed
light another cigarette.
Hooning cars,
barking dogs.
Drivers
think my street
is the Indianapolis 500
I'm sure.

45. Seamless boundaries

Seamless boundaries
crossed time and time and time again.
imaginary promises, only one of us makes.
You are numb by the world.
I'm on fire—burning within without,
where is the world tonight?
Corpses on my lawn,
skeletons in my desk.

Dreams withheld just long enough
for us to love again.
where are you tonight?
will you ever think of me?

Seamless suits of skin.
needle unthreads all of us.
And time becomes just
another reason to ransom away our rhymes.
seamless borders.

Confusing the situation even greater tonight.
light a cigarette.
drink more vodka.
my only true companions in the night.

www.ingramcontent.com/pod-product-compliance
Ingram Content Group UK Ltd.
Pitfield, Milton Keynes, MK11 3LW, UK
UKHW020234250726
13967UKWH00001B/363